BECAUSE WE LOVE

Our Planet. Our Wildlife. Our Future.

FIONA GOULDING

First Published 2026 by
Redback Publishing
Suite 6, 13a Narabang Way,
Belrose NSW 2085
Australia

www.redbackpublishing.com
email: info@redbackpublishing.com

ISBN: 978-1-761400-04-9

Author: Fiona Goulding
Illustrator: Fiona Goulding

NATIONAL LIBRARY OF AUSTRALIA
A catalogue record for this book is available from the National Library of Australia

Millions of creatures roam this Earth
and all of us have equal worth.
We all need food and shelter too;
few can adapt, but not all do.
So if our climate changes more,
some won't keep up, affecting us all...

unless

we work together, we rise above,
we protect wildlife,
because we love...

Polar bears use the floating sea ice
to hunt for food; nothing else will suffice.
If warm oceans melt these platforms away
it will become harder to hunt for their prey.
Without enough food to last them all year,
will these mighty creatures just disappear?

Snow leopards love their alpine home;
there among cliffs and ravines they roam.
As temperatures rise, so do the treelines.
Glaciers melt and their food source declines.
If alpine habitats continue to shrink,
how could these big cats adapt, do you think?

With striking wings of orange and black,
monarch butterflies migrate far north and back.
Temperature is used as their cue to take flight;
there'll be food on arrival if their timing is right.
But if warmer climates disrupt this migration,
will they find food and a home for hibernation?

The **giant panda** thrives in bamboo!
It provides food, water and shelter too.
But if climates get warmer, humidity lasts longer,
rainfall increases and flooding gets stronger!
What then are giant pandas to do,
if landslides and floods destroy the bamboo?

Burrowed in earth, eggs nestle together,
waiting for their gender that's determined by weather.
Warm soils produce more **tuatara** males,
with prominent spines, on their backs and their tails.
If only male reptiles grow to adulthood,
will the species survive? What's the likelihood?

Elephants need lots of water to drink.
Up to 50 gallons a day! That's a lot, don't you think?
They use water to hydrate, to keep cool and to play,
sucking water with their trunks to drink or to spray!
If a warm climate sends water into the sky,
what will they do when the earth is all dry?

With camouflage so clever, the **snowshoe hare**
sheds furs to change colour, so you can't see it's there.
Every winter it turns white, to blend with the snow,
and in summer it's brown, with the light's golden glow.
But if temperatures rise, and snow melts too fast,
will the hare's fur and the land be in contrast?

There are six snowshoe hares hiding, can you see? Spot them in the snow, or the shadow of the tree.

Koalas spend their days in tall green trees,
sleeping and nibbling on eucalyptus leaves.
If too much carbon dioxide harms the atmosphere,
it alters these leaves; the effects are severe.
When leaf toxins increase, koalas beware!
You might need to find food and water elsewhere.

Kiwi have nostrils at the end of their beak
to sniff out the insects and worms that they seek.
If the Earth gets warmer and the soil keeps drying,
will the poor kiwi stop digging and trying?
What happens when they can't pierce the tough ground?
Will all of their food remain hidden ... unfound?

Fairy terns lay eggs in a scrape in the sand
so that coastal foods are close at hand.
Hidden amongst shells of grey and white,
it's easy to spot predators day or night.
But if harsh climates bring storms and high tides,
will their young be exposed to threats from all sides?

Puffins catch fish by diving deep in the sea.
They 'fly' through the water with great energy!
Each year, they nest in the very same place,
and hope to find fish at this precious home base.
But what if the waters have started to heat?
If all the fish leave, what then can puffins eat?

Krill supports marine life on a massive scale.
They're food for many fish and the **humpback whale**.
For protection, krill swarm as a large red haze;
the ocean appears to be set ablaze.
If sea temperatures rise the krill can't survive.
How will the creatures that live off them thrive?

Beginning life as hatchlings, tiny on the land,
sea turtles race towards the sea over the sand.
Travelling long distances, the females lay their spawn
at the same nesting site, where they too were born.
Eggs are buried in the sand to hide them from pests.
Would extreme storms and tides destroy their safe nests?

In saltwater mangrove swamps, **Bengal tigers** thrive.
As these flood often, how do mangroves survive?
With ways to filter salt and with freshwater stores,
and roots above water which breathe through special pores.
But if sea levels rise and the mangroves can't breathe,
this habitat will die, the precious tigers will leave.

Should we let wildlife just disappear?
Does climate action matter? Is it yet clear?
The elephants, the whale, the tuatara?
The fairy tern, kiwi, puffin and koala?
The turtle, the leopard, the polar bear?
Pandas, monarch butterflies, tiger and hare?
I believe that we really do care!
We can work together. We can rise above.
We can protect wildlife,
because we love!